Silver Seal's Adventures

Ice Rescue

Diana Williams

Illustrations by André Haudiquet

Brighstone
Publishing

Brighstone Publishing
7 Maybank Gardens, Pinner HA5 2JW
www.brighstonepublishing.com

Printed and bound in the UK

ISBN: 978-0-9564158-1-3

A catalogue record of this book is available from the British Library.

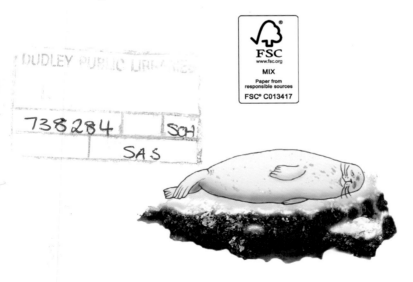

FSC
www.fsc.org
MIX
Paper from
responsible sources
FSC® C013417

A big thank you to Marianne, Bill, Jenny, Teresita and Judy for their guidance and support, and to André for his lovely pictures.

The sighting of a seal on a warm summer's evening at Worbarrow Bay in Dorset led to the creation of the Silver Seal stories. Since then, I have been lucky to have had more seal encounters.

The most recent was on Loch Melfort in the West of Scotland. A young seal decided to follow me as I kayaked across the loch. Every now and then, he would pop his head up and give me an intense stare. Thrilled to have his company, I decided to tell him a little about Silver. Did he understand? Probably not — though he seemed interested enough.

I can't wait to see more seals. Who knows, one day I might get to see the original Silver again.

Ice Rescue

Silver was sprawled over a snow-covered rock. Snow flurries blew all around him. It was cold. Very cold! How he would love to feel the warm sun on his back. He thought briefly of his good friend Cedric the turtle, who, at that moment, was probably swimming in the warm Caribbean Sea.

Still, he shouldn't complain; he was on his way to visit his family. He hadn't seen them for a long time and was really looking forward to it. Before he continued his journey though, he needed some rest. The rock was comfortable enough, and the snow gave it extra padding. Silver gave a huge yawn and shut his eyes.

"Er, what's that? What, er?" Silver awoke suddenly to a sharp shrilling. At first, he couldn't see anything, just snow and a wild sea. Then he looked down. Just below him, on a shelf jutting out from the rock, was a puffin. His brightly coloured beak shone out against the snowy white surroundings.

"They said that I might find you here," cried the bird.

"They?" questioned Silver.

"Dilly Dolphin and her friends. They told me, if ever there is a problem, find Silver. He'll know what to do." The puffin flapped his wings to shake off the snow.

"Problem?"

"Yes — it's a big one. I can't understand it. I've never seen it before." The puffin's words gushed out.

"Tell me," said Silver calmly.

The puffin took a deep breath and said, "It's the bears — they're stuck on the ice."

"Stuck on the ice? Bears?"

"Yes — the polar bears. They're stuck."

Silver was confused. Didn't polar bears live on ice? How could they be stuck?

The puffin explained further. "They are stuck on an ice floe with no food. There's no other ice close to them. There are young ones too — if they try to swim to the pack ice where they can hunt, they probably won't make it."

This was serious! Silver normally kept away from polar bears – after all they ate seals – but he didn't like to think of any of his fellow creatures in trouble. What was happening to the ice? Silver had a feeling that the two-legged ones might have something to do with this, but there was no time to ponder on the causes. He had to find a way to help the bears.

The puffin looked at Silver expectantly.

"Hmmm — I need to think for a bit," he told the bird.

The puffin nodded. "I'm John, by the way," he said.

"Pleased to meet you," Silver answered, before returning to his thoughts. This was a difficult one. How was he going to get the polar bears off the ice floe? He gazed out towards the horizon. Perhaps the sea would give him some inspiration.

Just then, a tall misty spray shot out of the choppy sea. A few seconds later, a huge head appeared. The huge head wore a huge smile. Silver shook his flippers with delight. It was his friend Felicity — the fin whale.

"Haven't seen you in these parts for a long while," said Felicity Fin Whale to Silver.

"No, I'm becoming a bit of a warm weather seal these days," he replied.

"With all that blubber?" joked Felicity.

Silver laughed. Then his face took on a more serious expression.

"What's up?" asked Felicity.

"You might just be the solution to a difficult problem," Silver said carefully.

John Puffin looked at Silver expectantly. Did he have a plan?

"Problem?" questioned Felicity.

Silver quickly explained about the polar bears.

"That's awful," cried the whale. "But what could I do?"

"Carry them to safety," answered Silver, marvelling at Felicity's good timing.

"Carry them to safety? Me? How would I do that?"

"I know!" shrieked John, unable to contain his excitement. "You could carry them on your back!"

"A polar bear on my back?!" Felicity thought the idea was ridiculous.

Silver had to admit that the idea did sound a little peculiar.

"It's the only way," Silver replied. "You're the only one big enough to do it."

"But what if they don't want to get on my back?" Felicity also knew that polar bears were good hunters, and had been known to attack some whales. What if one of them decided to try and eat her?

"I'll talk to them," volunteered John. "They know me."

"Humfph!" Felicity muttered.

Silver thought that it was a good idea for John to go and talk to them. He was the most capable of escape if the polar bears decided that they needed a snack.

"Please help us," Silver said to Felicity.

"Ohh – okay then – only as it's you who's asking," she replied, "but I won't hesitate to throw them off if one of them decides to take a bite out of me."

"Right – let's go – show us the way," said Silver to John, before plunging into the icy cold water.

John took off into the air and began circling above Silver and the whale. "Yes — let's go," he shrilled.

"I'll give you a ride," said Felicity to Silver. "It'll be practice for carrying those furry creatures."

Felicity dived down into the water. As she re-surfaced, Silver found himself rising up on her back.

"Hold on," the whale said, as she started to move through the water, following the puffin flying above.

Silver hung on tight. Felicity's back was quite slippery, and a couple of times he almost slid into the water. He hoped that the polar bears would manage to hang on.

Silver was very relieved when the polar bears were in sight. It didn't feel right, a seal riding on a whale's back.

Slipping into the water, he began to take stock of the situation. It was no longer snowing, and the bears were easy to see.

Three of them – a mother and two cubs – stood on the edge of a large floating piece of ice.

The mother looked very worried and, every now and then, would stand on her hind legs and give a panic-stricken cry.

The cubs, unaware of their mother's anxiety, continued to play — tumbling and rolling around each other. Often, the cubs would come close to falling into the water, and the mother would push them back with a large paw.

"There are two more of them." shrilled John, as he landed on Felicity's back. "Over there!" He pointed his wing in the direction of another mother bear with one cub. These bears were calmer than the others, and were standing dolefully on the edge of the ice. It was clear that they also had no idea what to do.

Silver felt extremely sad. He knew that if they did not get the bears to an area where they could find food, the cubs might not survive. There were no colonies of seals or walruses in this area for them to eat. Seals! Silver shivered. Still, as he told himself, every animal has to eat something. Unfortunately, polar bears liked eating his kind.

Felicity had parked herself close to Silver. As she looked at the polar bear mother who was standing upright crying out, Felicity said, "I don't fancy carrying that one — or her cubs."

Silver could understand why, but he had to remain positive. "I'm sure she'll be fine. She's just a bit worried at the moment."

"Humfph," muttered Felicity.

"Right then," said Silver, taking charge of the situation, "John, you said you'd speak to them. Go and tell them our plan."

John Puffin took off in the bears' direction.

"Be careful!" shouted Silver after him.

John decided to visit the calmer polar bears first. Just as he was about to land, the cub leapt at him. All John could see were massive paws heading in his direction. He just made it into the air in time. This was going to be harder than he thought. Flapping his wings as hard as he could to keep in the air, he decided to talk to the mother bear from above. The cub was now on his hind legs trying to swipe at him, so John had to keep a decent height.

"I've brought someone to help you — to get you to safety."

The mother bear let out a terrible roar. John hoped that she wasn't eyeing him up for their next meal.

"I've come to help you," John tried again.

Silver had been watching; John's efforts were not going that well. He decided to speak to the bears himself. Swimming closer to them, but keeping a safe distance, Silver called out, "We can get you to where there's food."

At the mention of food, the cub stopped jumping, and the mother's ears pricked up to listen. The large seal talking to her looked very tasty!

Sensing danger, Silver decided to make a little more space between him and the bears.

"We've arranged transport for you," shrilled John from above.

"Transport?" Interested in hearing more, the mother turned her attention from the big and juicy-looking seal in the water.

At that moment, an island appeared. A jet of mist and vapour soared from it — a whale's blow. It was Felicity!

She stuck her head out of the water and looked directly at the polar bear.

"Here's your transport," called out Silver. "Felicity will carry you to safety."

"A whale! Carry us?!" The bear, who was now looking at Felicity, gave a scornful laugh.

"Yes," said Silver, "that is if you want help. I would not want to be stuck here with nothing to eat. There are no seal colonies around, and I doubt your cub could swim far enough to find them."

The bear became quiet. She was obviously considering the matter.

John called to Silver from above. It was a warning; the other polar bears were coming over. Silver hoped that there would not be a fight. Polar bears were not always that friendly with their own kind. The mother that they had been talking to had also noticed them. She stood on her hind legs and gave a growl to the others to keep away.

"John, fly over to them — tell them what we are trying to do."

With a nod, he headed in their direction. This time he did not attempt to land. The cubs had already lined him up as something to swat and play with.

Silver spoke again. "If I were you, I would accept our help. If you stay here, you might even have to fight for your ground. You could lose your cub."

That was it; the mother did not want to lose her cub at any cost. After so little food, she did not have much energy left. She might not be strong enough to protect him.

"Okay," she said. "How do we get on?"

"Just wait here — Felicity will pull alongside the ice."

"And don't bite me," called out Felicity, just before she moved herself into position. "If you do, you'll be straight in the water!"

The bear nodded and picked her cub up by the neck. The cub gave a few cries — what was happening? What was this giant creature that had pulled up alongside them? The mother stepped carefully onto Felicity's back. The whale felt slimy. Ooops — she slipped. The cub whimpered; it didn't want to end up in the water. Grasping Felicity's flipper, the mother managed to cling on and haul herself back up. She kept the cub in her mouth. She wasn't going to let go of him.

Silver gave a cheer as Felicity headed off in the direction of polar bear food, and safe ice.

The polar bear just managed to lift a paw, a thank you to Silver and John. Hopefully, she'd go a little easier on seals in the future!

Meanwhile, the other polar bears were looking on with amazement. A polar bear and its cub riding a whale?! It couldn't be!

John shrilled to them, "We can help you too! Get you to safety!"

The mother polar bear looked at John suspiciously. "What if the whale decides to eat my cubs?" she said grumpily.

"Don't worry, Felicity only eats things like fish and krill," answered John.

The second polar bear mother looked at her cubs. Like the first mother, she was desperate to keep her offspring safe. If she had to ride a whale to achieve this, then so be it.

"Okay — I'll do it."

"Great," said John. "Felicity will be back soon and then she'll take you. We have the next set of passengers!" he called to Silver.

All of a sudden, there was a creaking, splitting sound. John looked down — the ice on which the three polar bears were standing was breaking up.

"Get back!" he called to the bears. "Get back!"

The mother polar bear quickly pushed back the closest cub and reached for the other one. It was too late; the ice had split right in front of her. Now one of the cubs was separated from its mother — stuck on a very small piece of ice, floating free.

The cub cried out in anguish. The mother gave a huge roar — a warning to stay put. The cub wanted to get back to its mother, and stood on its hind legs, its front paw reaching out to her.

"Stay still," the mother called out, just as the cub lost its balance and fell headlong into the water. What was the mother to do? Should she jump in and rescue her cub? What about the other cub? What if he fell in too? Thrashing around in the cold water, the cub was just about managing to keep afloat. Scared and confused, it was clear that she needed some help. The cub went under. That was it. Now the mother had no choice, and she began to enter the water.

"Stay there!" cried John urgently. "Stay there!" He had noticed something that the mother bear had not.

The cub's head popped up to the surface again. Calmer now, it was almost as though she was resting in the water. Below the bear was a dark shadow. Something was helping the little bear to stay afloat! John knew what it was. It was Silver!

"Silver's got her," he told the mother. "Don't worry, Silver's got her!"

Just as Silver was about to nudge the cub towards the ice, Felicity returned. Coming up below them, she lifted Silver and the cub out of the water.

"Hold on tight to Felicity," Silver told the cub, as he slipped off her back, into the sea.

Satisfied that her cub was alright, the polar bear mother took her remaining cub in her mouth, whilst waiting for Felicity to pull up alongside. This cub was very wriggly, and the mother gave a few gentle growls from behind her closed teeth to get him to behave.

"I told you I didn't like the look of this bunch," grumbled Felicity to Silver.

"They'll be fine," Silver reassured her. "They're just scared."

"Humfph," replied Felicity.

Silver was right, their ride to the pack ice went as smoothly as it had done for the first bears.

Amazed, and perhaps a little scared, to be riding on a whale's back, the cubs kept very still — one now on its mother's back, the other secure in her mouth. This time, Silver swam alongside them, whilst John perched on Felicity. Pulling up close to the ice, it was fantastic for Silver, John and, of course, Felicity to watch the bears step to safety. Now, at last, they should be able to find some food.

"Hurrah!!" cried John Puffin and, to celebrate, Felicity Fin Whale lifted her tail, sending a fountain of water into the air.

Polar bears are beautiful creatures, Silver thought. They deserve to survive.

Putting her cubs down, the bear called out, "I'll never forget this. I'll tell everyone I meet how you helped us."

"It's our pleasure," said Silver, who then proceeded to thank John and Felicity warmly, before saying goodbye.

Silver then remembered that he was on his way to visit his family. Still, it had been a busy morning, and the rock he had been snoozing on earlier was not too far away.

A little rest before he headed off again would be the perfect thing. As he settled himself down on the snowy rock, Silver cast his mind back over the day's events.

It had been a good result – the polar bears were now free to roam and find food – although he still felt uneasy. Why was the ice floe that the polar bears had been rescued from so far away from any others? When he had travelled this way before, he had seen a lot of ice floes, all quite close together.

It was obvious that the polar bears hadn't expected to be stuck so far away from their hunting grounds. What was going on? If only he could find some answers. He remembered an earlier thought. The two-legged ones! Did they have anything to do with the polar bears' problems? Silver gave a huge yawn, and his eyes started to close.

Entering the world of dreams, he found himself back in the sea, swimming in circles around Felicity Fin Whale. Every now and again, she would flick her tail gently in his direction and send him spinning. John Puffin kept diving down to watch. There was nothing to worry about, they were just having fun.

Helping Marine Life

There are many individuals and groups that care about the marine world and are working hard to protect it. Polar Bears International, the Hebridean Whale and Dolphin Trust and the Scottish Seabird Centre all gave their expert advice for the following facts pages. You can find out more about these organisations and the work that they do by going to their websites:

www.polarbearsinternational.org

www.HWDT.org

www.seabird.org

Global Warming

Silver could not understand why there was so little ice around the polar bears. We know, however, that this is linked to global warming, which is a rise in the temperature of the earth's atmosphere. The earth takes in heat from the sun and, like a greenhouse, keeps some of the heat, before letting the rest back through the atmosphere and into space.

An increased build up of greenhouse gases, such as carbon dioxide and methane, that trap heat in the atmosphere, has meant that less heat is escaping and the earth is warming up. The increase in greenhouse gases is largely due to our activities, including industrial processes and burning fossil fuels like coal and oil.

Global warming can also cause flooding. As the ice melts, the sea level will rise, threatening the low-lying coastal areas of the world. Changes in the weather are also likely to occur. Some places could experience hotter summers and more rainy winters, whilst other countries may experience less rain – leading to drought.

Changes in rainfall and temperature affect how our crops (food) grow, which could result in some countries not having enough food.

Plants and animals have become used to the conditions in the parts of the world where they live, and the change that global warming brings will affect their ability to exist. In the case of the polar bears, the sea ice from which they normally feed is melting, retreating in summer further and further off shore. Adult polar bears are good swimmers, but undertaking long journeys to reach the ice can leave them exhausted and unable to cope with the very cold water and large waves. There is evidence that some bears have drowned.

As people, we have an important challenge ahead. It's not just a matter of adapting our lives to deal with climate change; we will have to work harder to reduce this problem.

Polar Bear Facts

Polar bears are the largest land carnivores (meat eaters) in the world. Preferring cold environments, there are estimated to be between 20,000 and 25,000 polar bears living within the Arctic Circle and its surrounding seas and land masses. Much of their time is spent on the sea ice and at sea, hunting seals that make up most of their diet. In the summer the bears follow the retreating ice, and the seals. Those polar bears that get stuck on land in the summer have to stay where they are, and wait until the ice begins to form again in the autumn. It is much harder for the polar bear to obtain sufficient food on land, and it is uncommon for them to catch seals in open water.

Polar bears normally live to around 25 years, although we know that one wild bear lived up to 32 years. Male polar bears can weigh up to 680kg and a female is roughly half that weight. Their legs are stocky, and their ears and tail are small. They have large feet to help them to walk on ice and to swim. The pads on their feet are covered with small, soft papillae (small bumps) to enable them to grip the ice. Short claws are useful for gripping their prey and, like the papillae, also help them to move easily on the ice. To protect themselves from the cold, polar bears have good insulation – up to 10cm of blubber (fat).

Polar bear fur is made up of a dense under-fur, and an outer layer of guard hairs. Their fur may look white, but it is actually transparent. A hollow core in the hair shaft scatters and reflects the light around it. Polar bears look their whitest in sunlight, particularly after the moulting period (usually spring to late summer). Before shedding their fur, their coat can look yellow due to the oils from the seals that they eat.

In terms of reproduction, polar bears mate on the sea ice in April and May. When the ice floes break up in autumn, the pregnant female digs a maternity den, often in a snow drift. Born in winter, the cubs are blind at birth. On average, each litter has two cubs. The family leave the den in the spring. Cubs are normally looked after by their mothers for two and a half years, after which the mother chases them away to fend for themselves.

Dangers to Polar Bears

As well as global warming, other threats to the polar bear are hunting and pollution. Oil and gas exploration and extraction can have a damaging effect on their habitat.

Fin Whale Facts

The fin whale is the world's second largest whale, and can grow up to 27 metres in length and weigh up to 120,000kg. Amongst the fastest of the great whales, it can reach a speed of 37km per hour. It is also able to dive to depths of 250 metres. The current fin whale population is estimated to be about 33,000.

Fin whales have streamlined bodies, with 'V' shaped heads that are flat on top. They are black or brownish grey in colour with a white underside. Perhaps the fin whale's main distinguishing feature is the colouring on its lower jaw, which is white or whitish-yellow on the right side and mottled black on the left.

For their food, fin whales favour schooling fish, squid and animal plankton, including krill (small prawn-like creatures). The pleated and expandable grooves in their throat allow them to take in large volumes of food and water. As the mouth closes, the water is pushed out through the baleen plates leaving the food trapped behind them. Hanging from each side of the upper jaw, these plates - made from keratin - fray out into fine hairs near the tongue.

Fin whales can be found in most regions of the world, but they do not often go where there is sea ice. Felicity Fin Whale, however, had good reason to head further north – she needed to save the polar bears.

In terms of reproduction, the fin whale's pregnancy lasts about 11 months. Calves are believed to be born at 3 to 4 year intervals and at birth will weigh between 1000kg and 1500kg. They will be nursed by their mothers for 6 to 8 months.

Fin whales can live for a long time. The oldest captured fin whale had reached an age of 111 years.

Puffin Facts

Puffins are seabirds, which breed in large colonies, mainly in burrows on coastal cliffs or on offshore islands. Members of the family of auks, there are three species of puffin – the Atlantic puffin, the tufted puffin and the horned puffin. John is an Atlantic puffin, and his kind is found in the North Atlantic Ocean.

In the breeding season, puffins have brightly coloured beaks. After breeding, they shed the colourful outer parts of their bill, leaving a smaller and duller beak. They are stocky in build and their feathers are mainly black and white. In flight, flapping their wings up to 400 times per minute, they can reach speeds of 88 km per hour.

Atlantic puffins catch their prey by flying underwater. Using their stubby wings, they swim down powerfully, whilst their webbed feet point them, like a rudder, in the right direction. They typically hunt small fish such as sandeels, sprats and herring, as well as crustaceans and molluscs.

When it comes to reproduction, one egg is laid each year and the parents take turns to incubate it. It takes 39-45 days for the egg to hatch, and the parents share the feeding of their single chick. Puffins can live up to twenty years, if not more.

Words and Music Stage Two

Ian Lawrence
Pamela Montgomery

Longman

LONGMAN GROUP LIMITED
London
*Associated companies, branches and representatives throughout
the world*

© Longman Group Ltd 1971

First published 1971
ISBN 0 582 18692 7

*Printed in Great Britain by Lowe & Brydone (Printers) Ltd,
London NW*10

*We are grateful to the following for permission to reproduce
photographs*
Barnaby's Picture Library, page 63 by Frederika Davis;
British Waterways Board, pages 24 and 25; Camera
Press Ltd, page 8; Fox Photos Ltd, page 36; Keystone
Agency Ltd, page 5; Radio Times Hulton Picture
Library, page 44.

*We are grateful to the following for permission to reproduce
copyright material*
The Clarendon Press for 'Three Jovial Huntsmen' and
'a rhyme' from *An Anthology of Verse for Children*, edited
by James Britton. The verse from 'The Lone Star Trail'
on page 41 is from *The American Song Book*, compiled
by J. Horton, E. J. Arnold.

Illustrations are by David Featherstone.

Note for Teachers

The use of '*An Introduction to Words and
Music*' is an essential accompaniment to this
book.

Contents

1 The Two Kings

Once upon a time, many years ago, in a land beyond seven mountains there lived two brothers. They were twins and were always quarrelling. When their father, the King, died he left a will. In the will he left half his kingdom to each son.

They fought many battles because each son wanted to be king of the whole kingdom. Soon there were only a few people left living in the land. The winter came and it was very cold. Everything was turned to ice. No birds sang. The people were hungry. They were tired of the two kings who were always fighting and never looking after the land.

They all met in the forest and decided to cross over the mountains into another land, where it would be peaceful and where there would be food.

They got ready for the journey and set off tramping through the snow. They sang to keep themselves going.

Trudge, trudge, trudge, trudge,
On we go
Through the snow.
Tramp, tramp, tramp, tramp,
No more fights,
Food to eat.
Trudge, trudge, trudge, trudge.
Trudge, trudge, trudge.

After several hours they came to a narrow pass in the mountains. Suddenly there was a loud roar. They looked up and saw an avalanche of snow rolling down the mountain

4

side. They ran and
sheltered in a cave.
When all was quiet,
they looked out. Snow
blocked the entrance
to the cave. They were
trapped.

Meanwhile back in
their castles the two
kings were surprised
to find that everyone
had left them. They
met each other, and for
once they forgot to
quarrel. There wasn't
much point in arguing
about the kingdom if
there were no people
living in the kingdom.
They decided to
follow the tracks in
the snow.

Do you think the two
kings found their
people?

How do you think
the story ends?

This is the rhythm of the song:

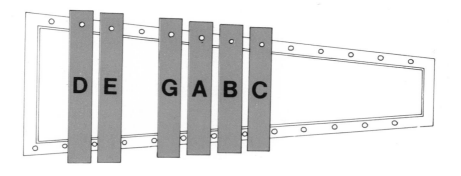

Trudge, trudge, trudge, trudge, On we go Through the snow

Tramp, tramp, tramp, tramp, No more fights Food to eat

Trudge, trudge, trudge, trudge, trudge, trudge, trudge.

These are the notes that we can use for the tune:

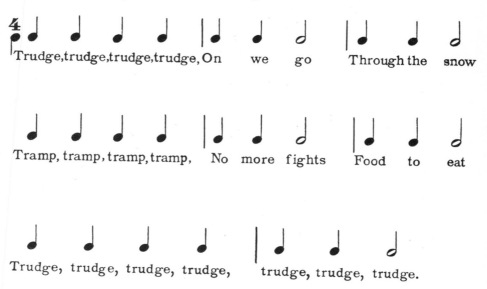

D E G A B C

You do not have to use all these notes. You may want to use only three or four of them.

When you have made a tune for the song, sing it all together a few times. Try singing it loudly, and try singing it quietly. Then try to sing it like this: start quietly, get louder in the middle and then get quieter again.

Do you think it sounds like the crowd coming towards you, then passing you and going on its way?

Can you play these notes on your recorders?

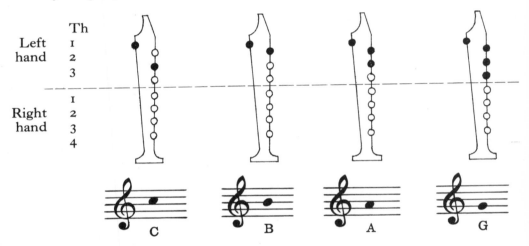

Here is a tune for you to play in your story:

Add parts for drums, tambourines, triangles and any other percussion instruments you have.

7

2 The Car Factory

'Quickly Bob, run after your Dad with his dinner-tin! He went off in such a rush that he left it behind.'

Bob ran and got his bike from the shed. He jumped on it

and rode down the narrow road to the factory. There were many people on bicycles, all rushing to work. A siren hooted and the cyclists pedalled faster.

Pedal, pedal, pedal faster
We're all very late!
Pedal, pedal, pedal faster
It's gone half-past eight!

Bob rode into the factory yard. He was hidden from the gate-keeper by the crowds of people. In the yard there were rows and rows of shiny new cars. Two men were walking towards him. He ducked behind a car and kept very still.

All was quiet. Bob ran over to the workshop where his father worked.

As he opened the door there was a roar of sound. The workshop was filled with many machines all running at high speed.

'You're not allowed in here!' It was the foreman. Bob explained and handed over the tin for his father. The foreman told him to go home quickly.

On his way out Bob saw a green sports car. He jumped in it and pretended to be a famous racing-driver. Then he heard voices, so he hid behind the back seat. He felt the car being moved. Later he looked out of the window. He saw that the car was on top of a large lorry, and the lorry was whizzing out into the country.

What happens to Bob?

This is the rhythm of the song:

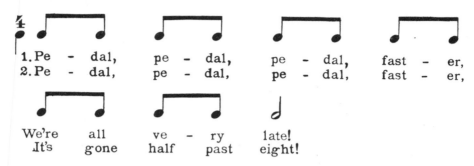

1. Pe - dal,   pe - dal,   pe - dal,   fast - er,
2. Pe - dal,   pe - dal,   pe - dal,   fast - er,

We're   all   ve - ry   late!
It's   gone   half past   eight!

These are the notes that we can use for the song:

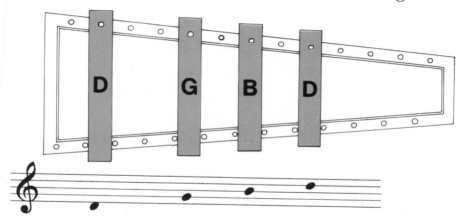

When Bob opens the door to the workshop he hears the sound of all the machines working. We can make some machinery music with our instruments. Collect all the instruments together and find out what interesting sounds they can make that remind you of the noises of a factory. Remember that machines usually work in a very rhythmic way. Perhaps some of you can form a group that makes the movements of a big machine.

Here is a new note for the recorders:

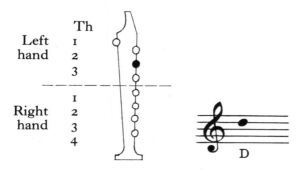

Now we have **five** notes that we can play:

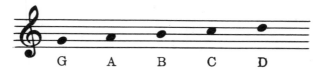

Here are two tunes using all five notes. You can use them in your story.

3 Olaf, the Viking

In 1014 Olaf, a Norwegian Viking, sailed to England with a fleet of these ships. Olaf was helping King Ethelred of England to capture London from the Danes.

The ships were strong and light. They could be rowed up shallow rivers or sail across the rough open seas. There were thirty-two oars in each boat. The men would sit on wooden chests to row.

It was a stormy crossing. The men rowed hard and sang songs.

When they landed on the south-east coast of England they had a fierce battle. One of the Viking leaders was killed in the battle. He was laid in his boat with his helmet, cloak, shield and sword. The boat was pushed out to sea. The Vikings shot flaming arrows through the air which landed on

12

the boat. As the blazing ship sank into the waves the Vikings
sang:

> Valkyries, Valkyries. Take him to Valhalla.
> He is brave. He is strong. Odin, Odin, hear our cries.

The Vikings waited until it was dark. Then they quietly
rowed up the river Thames. Some of the men climbed overboard and swam up to London Bridge. They tied ropes to
the wooden posts which kept the bridge up.

The other ends were tied to the boats. Olaf gave the order
to row. With fierce cries they rowed as hard as they could.
The bridge came crashing down. Now that the bridge was
down, the ships with their tall masts were able to sail into
London. The battle was won.

This is the rhythm of the Viking song:

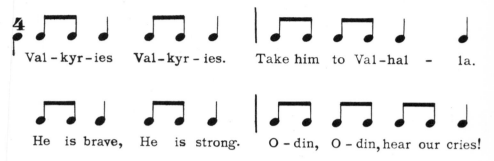

Val - kyr - ies   Val - kyr - ies.   Take him to Val - hal - la.

He is brave, He is strong.   O - din, O - din, hear our cries!

These are the notes that we can use for the tune:

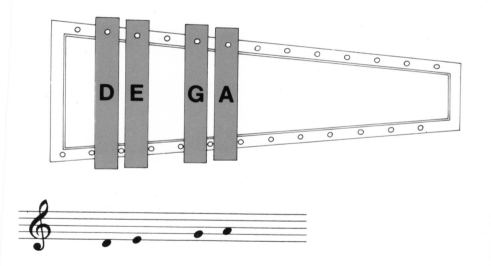

After they had won the battle, the Vikings naturally took the first opportunity to celebrate their victory. At the feast they had some music. This is how it started:

Can you continue it?

You could use the same two chords all the way through, and use only the notes G, A, B, C and D on your recorders.

Here are two more tunes for the recorders that you can use in the story:

Add parts for percussion instruments when you are sure you can play these tunes.

A Knight and a Lady

A knight and a lady
Went one day
Far into the forest
  Away, away.

'Fair knight,' said the lady,
'I pray, have a care.
This forest is evil;
  Beware, beware.'

A fiery red dragon
They spied on the grass;
The lady wept sorely,
  Alas! Alas!

The knight slew the dragon,
The lady was gay,
They rode on together
  Away, away.

ANON.

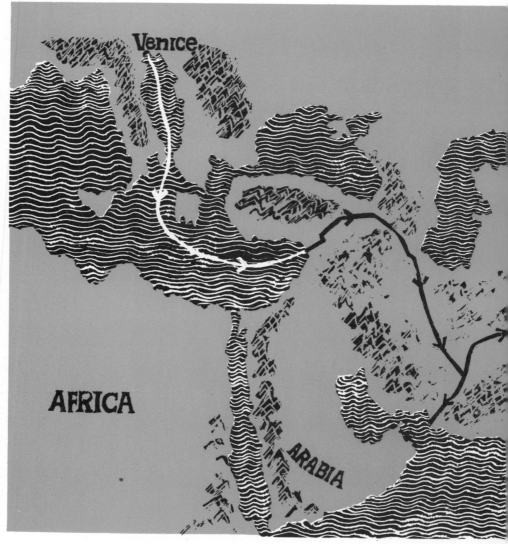

In 1271 Marco Polo, a young man, sailed from Venice with his father and uncle. They were to go thousands of miles to meet the famous Genghis Khan in China.

18

After crossing the Himalayas they reached a desert. It was wild country and they were afraid of robbers. They were glad when they saw a long caravan coming. There were yaks, camels, ponies loaded with food, spices and water. The leader of the caravan said that they could travel with them.

At night they made huge fires. The women cooked meat and the men danced, clapped and sang to the beat of drums. Marco Polo sat with the leader and his family enjoying the feasts.

One day there was a sandstorm. The sand swirled around them. They lay down and covered their faces. Then they heard strange singing.

You who come here
You will die.

You who come here
Never will return.

It was the Caraunas, a fierce robber tribe. They sang to frighten the people, so that they could steal their goods. But the leader of the caravan helped the Polos. He told them to tie themselves underneath their camels. The camels galloped away and the robbers didn't see them. The rest of the people died of thirst in the desert.

There are three places in this story where music can help to add to the excitement:
1   When the long caravan arrives in the desert.
2   When they are having their feast at night.
3   The frightening tune sung by the Caraunas.

The arrival of the caravan

We can make a tune for the recorders to play, and the drums and other percussion instruments can accompany it. Have you ever heard a band marching towards you? At first it sounds very quiet, but as it gets nearer it sounds louder and louder.

If we play the tune four times we could have:

First time: Very soft
Second time: Soft
Third time: Loud
Fourth time: Very loud

Remember that the camels are not *marching*: they seem to swing along at a steady, rather slow pace.
These are the notes that the recorders can use:

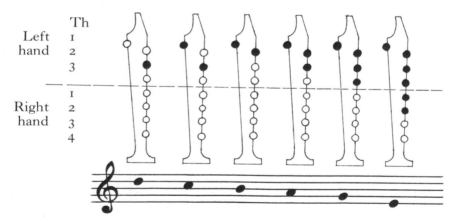

Remember that you do not have to use *all* these notes, but can choose which ones you want.

The feast music

These are the chime bar notes that we can use:

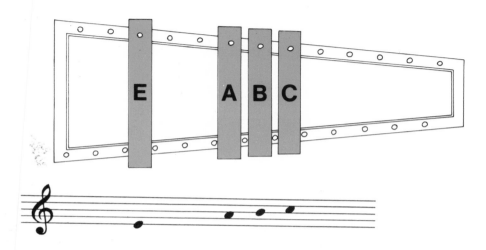

This is how the dance begins:

Can you continue it?

The song of the Caraunas

This is the rhythm of the song:

| You | who | come | here, | You | will | die. |

| You | who | come | here, | Ne - ver | will | re - turn. |

When you make a tune for the song, remember that it must be *frightening*.

23

5 Adventure on the Grand Trunk Canal

It is 1810. A family lives on this Narrow Boat on the Grand Trunk Canal. The boat is about seventy feet long and seven feet wide. It is made of wood and all the family live in a small cabin in the stern of the boat. They travel about twenty miles a day and are pulled along by a strong horse.

Today the boat reaches the Harecastle Old Tunnel. There is no towpath through the tunnel. Some of the children take the horse through the fields, and will meet the barge at the other end of the tunnel.

Inside the tunnel the family take it in turns to lie on the top of the boat. They push against the tunnel sides with

their feet. It is dark and the tunnel is nearly two miles long.
They sing:

> One, two, leg, leg,
> One, two, leg, leg.
> Into the dark we go.
> Into the dark we go.

They hear shouts! Another boat is coming through the
tunnel. They try to stop. But, too late! The boats bump into
each other. There is a splash! Someone is overboard!

This is the rhythm of the song:

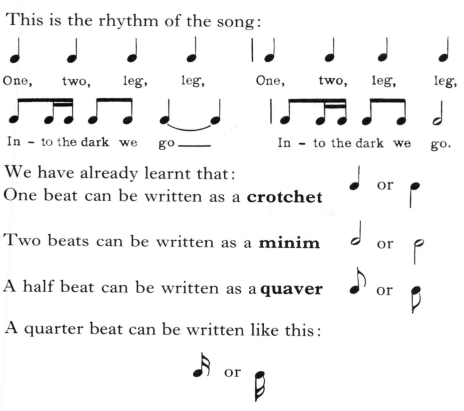

We have already learnt that:
One beat can be written as a **crotchet**

Two beats can be written as a **minim**

A half beat can be written as a **quaver**

A quarter beat can be written like this:

It is called a **semi-quaver**
Two semi-quavers are written like this:

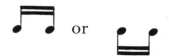

When two semi-quavers follow a quaver it is written like this:

These are the notes that we can use for the song:

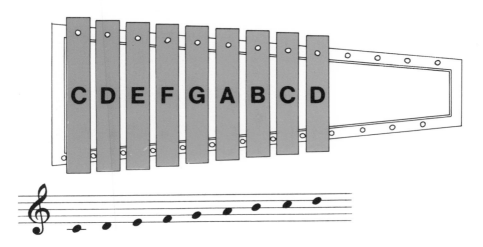

Choose a group of not more than five of these notes for your tune.

Can you clap these rhythms?

Choose one of the rhythms on page 27 to use for a recorder tune. When you have made a tune that you like, see if you can write it down. These are the recorder notes that you have learnt:

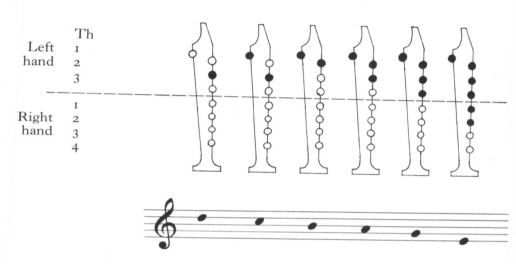

Of course, you do not have to use all the notes if you do not wish to.

6 Indian Tale: How Music came to the Earth

The North American Indians loved telling stories. In the winter, when the nights were long and dark they sat around their fire. The wind howled around their tipi and they listened to the story teller. This is a story told by the Flathead Tribe who lived in the Northern Rocky Mountains.

One day the Sun looked upon the people and saw that they were sad. The sun called Beaver and Coyote and said 'I have given the people everything that they need. Yet they are silent.'

Beaver and Coyote thought hard. Beaver and Coyote told the Sun that the people did not know how to make music. Without music the people were sad.

. Beaver and Coyote made a plan.

They crept into the tipi of a hunter and stole all his buffalo skins. The hunter was very angry. His family were very cold without the buffalo skins to keep them warm. He

29

went off with his friends to hunt more buffalo. After many days of tracking they found a bull elk and killed it.

They skinned the elk and built a great fire. As they were cooking the meat a large flame sprang out and burnt all the hair on the elk skin. The hunter threw away the skin. Beaver and Coyote crept out and spread the skin over an old hollow tree stump.

The hunter went out to hunt another elk. He hunted for many days. When he came back he saw the elk skin on the tree stump. He pulled it, but it was stuck and had dried to the tree stump. He pulled it again, but it was still stuck fast. In a temper he picked up a stick and beat the skin.

A strange noise came from the tree stump. It sounded like the sound of buffalo feet. He beat faster and faster. The people came running saying 'What is this wonderful sound?' They began to laugh and shout, clap and dance. Suddenly they were singing.

We dance and clap
We clap and sing,
And we love the beat
Just like buffalo feet.

We leap and jump
We clap and sing,
And we love the beat
Just like buffalo feet.

Beaver and Coyote stood in the forest and watched.
Then they also started to dance and sing:

So now they are glad
And no longer sad
And they love the beat
Just like buffalo feet.

The sun shone bright in the sky.
That is the tale told by the Flathead tribe.

This is the rhythm of the song:

We   dance and   clap, ⎫ We   clap   and   sing, And we
We   leap and   jump, ⎭

love   the   beat   just like   buf - fa - lo   feet.

And this is the rhythm of Beaver's and Coyote's song:

So   now they are glad and no   long - er   sad, And they

love   the   beat   just like   buf - fa - lo   feet.

Clap and say the words of both songs. Do you hear that they are very similar? Try saying them together. One group says the words of the first song while another group says the words of the other song. When you are making tunes for these songs, perhaps you would like to see if you can fit the two songs together.

These are the notes that we can use for the tunes:

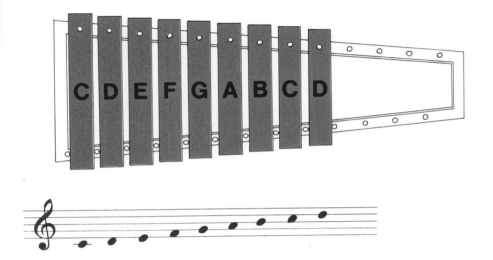

Remember that we do not *have* to use all of them if we do not want to.

Here are some rhythms that you could use to accompany the singers:

Here is another note for the recorders:

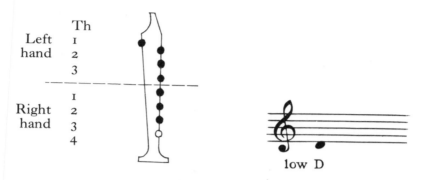

low D

And here is a tune to play in the story:

7 Indian Tale: How Fire came to the Earth

This is a tale told by the Nimipu tribe of Red Indians. They lived in the Rockie Mountains above the Clearwater river.

At the beginning of time, the Nimipu tribe had no fire. They ate raw fish, meat, berries and nuts. Without fire they were cold. They wore many skins to keep warm. But still they shivered.

There was a thunder storm and they looked up at the sky. The lightning flashed and the thunder roared. The Indians thought that the fire lived in the black thunder clouds. So they made special music to bring the fire down to earth. They beat their drums, sang and danced.

> Bright fire in the sky,
> Come down to us.
> Bright fire in the sky,
> Sink down to earth.

Soon the thunder storm passed. The Indians stopped singing and walked sadly back to their tipis. The fire had not come.

A young boy said 'I will bring down the fire'. They all laughed at him. 'How can you bring down the fire? We have made our fire music and still the fire stays in the sky!'

But when the next thunder storm came, the boy went to the top of a hill. He took his best bow and a long arrow. He wore a white shell around his neck. He put the shell on the ground and then shot his arrow high into the storm. It went so high that no one could see it.

35

The tribe watched him and thought he was a fool.

But the arrow fell burning in flames. It landed in the white shell and high flames shot out of it. The tribe rushed forward with sticks which they lit from the flames. They laughed and sang with joy.

Look, look, the fire has come!
The flames are hot,
The sparks are bright.
Look, look, the fire has come!

Later they looked for the boy to thank him. But he had gone. They looked everywhere. All they could find was the white shell.

That is the tale told by the Nimipu tribe of Red Indians.

This is the rhythm of the words of the first song:

This is the rhythm of the second song:

These are the notes that we can choose from for the two songs:

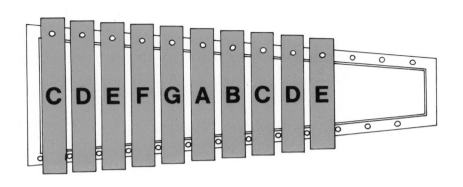

We do not have to use *all* the notes in either song. In the first song you might like to use only the notes

In the second song you might like to use only the notes

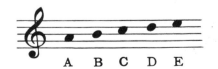

This tune for recorders can be played at the end of the story when the tribe is looking for the boy:

These are the notes that are used in the melody:

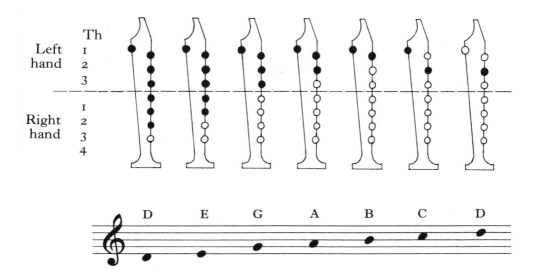

8 The Lone Star Trail

This is the flag of the State of Texas in the United States of America. Because there is a single star on the flag, Texas has

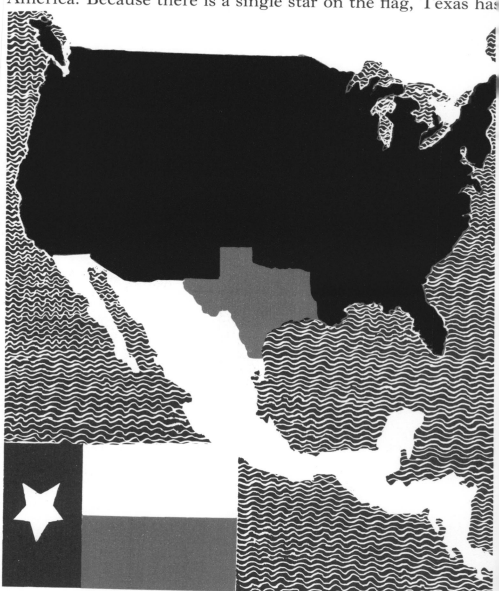

always been called the 'Lone Star State'. Texas is the biggest state in the U.S.A. (apart from Alaska, which is separated from the rest of the country). It is at the southern end of the U.S.A., next to the country of Mexico.

Today over ten million people live in Texas, and there are lots of big towns with factories and oil wells. But not so long ago cattle farming was almost the only work for the people living there. Cowboys had to ride across the wide, hot plains driving great herds of cattle from one feeding ground to another, or to market. On their long journeys the cowboys used to sing together about their work. One of these songs was called 'The Lone Star Trail'.

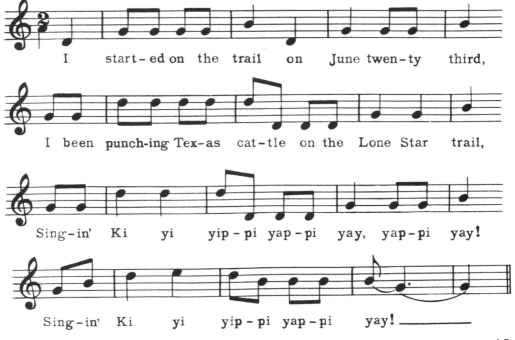

I start-ed on the trail on June twen-ty third,

I been punch-ing Tex-as cat-tle on the Lone Star trail,

Sing-in' Ki yi yip-pi yap-pi yay, yap-pi yay!

Sing-in' Ki yi yip-pi yap-pi yay! ___

Punching cattle means driving the herd across country.

Ki yi yippi yay are sounds used by the cowboys when they are rounding up the cattle.

These are the notes that are used in the song:

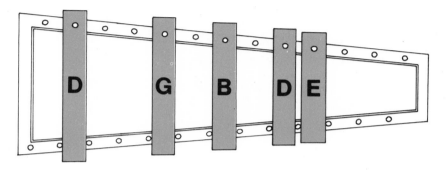

In order to play it on our recorders we must learn this new note:

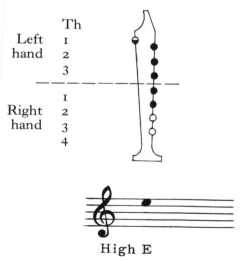

High E

For this note the left hand thumb covers only *half* the hole.

42

There are lots of verses in this song. The singers were always making up new ones. Can you make a verse of your own? Here is the rhythm of the song to help you:

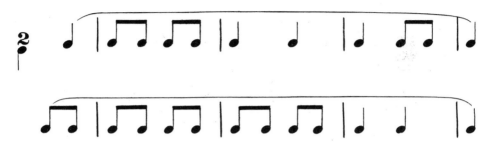

Singing Ki yi yippi *etc.*

If you would like to use the chime bars for an accompaniment to the tune, try using this two bar pattern:

G   A   B   D   E   D   B   A

For the last two bars you could end like this:

G   A   B   D   E   D   G

Now that we can sing and play the song, let us use it in a story about cowboys in Texas. Can you make up an exciting story of your own?

43

9 Treasure at the Bottom of the Sea

Professor Glum and Professor Gludge live on an island a few miles from Gloombolia. They have been busy for many years making a special machine to go to the bottom of the sea.

It has a plastic watertight dome which will cover the Professors and allow them to stay on the sea bed for many days. There are three propellors to move the machine through the water. On the bottom there are four steel feet so that it can walk along the sea bed. Sticking out there are two long steel arms which will be used for digging and lifting. There is also a harpoon gun to catch fish so that they can eat during their long stay on the sea bed.

At last the machine is ready. They plan to find an old galleon which lies many fathoms down. They are sure that

the old wreck contains many chests of Spanish gold. They hope to lift the timbers of the wreck. They climb into the machine, pull over the dome and start up the engine. It makes strange noises, then walks down the beach and disappears into the sea.

As soon as the machine has gone, a man climbs down from a tree from where he has been secretly watching what the professors have been doing. He runs across the beach, gets into a motor boat and speeds to the other side of the island. There is a yacht anchored in the bay.

Who is on board the yacht?

Is the treasure brought to the surface?

You can make the sounds of the machine with your voices and with your instruments:

1 Press dome button: dome closes

Zzzzz   Zzzzz   Zz Zz Zz Zz   Zzzzzzzzzzzzzzzzzzzz

2 Press starter button: engine starts

Can you make up the sounds for these rhythms? First try each rhythm by itself, then try all three rhythms together, dividing yourselves into three groups.

3 Pull switch to start mechanical feet:
Make sounds for this rhythm:

4 As the machine enters the water, start the propellers:
Can you make up the sounds *and* the rhythm?

46

The machine takes a long time to reach the bottom of the sea.
Make some sinking music for it while it goes down.

Use these notes:

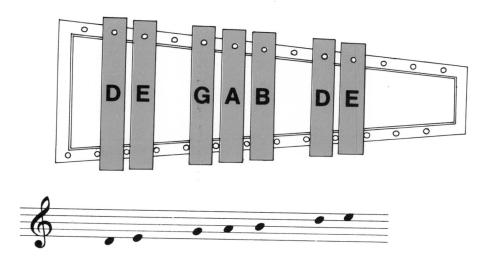

Here are two new notes for the recorders:

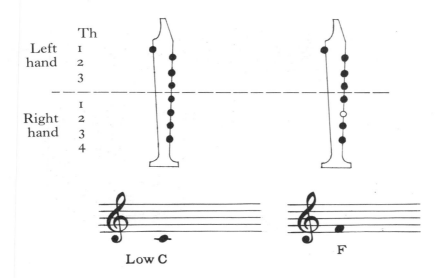

Low C   F

These are two tunes which use the two new notes. They can
be used in your story.

48

Three Jovial Huntsmen

There were three jovial huntsmen
As I have heard them say,
And they would go a-hunting
All on a summer's day.

All the day they hunted,
And nothing could they find
But a ship a-sailing
A-sailing with the wind.

One said it was a ship
The other said Nay;
The third said it was a house
With the chimney blown away.

And all the night they hunted
And nothing could they find;
But the moon a-gliding,
A-gliding with the wind.

One said it was the moon,
The other said Nay;
The third said it was a cheese,
And half of it cut away.

UNKNOWN.

10 Ulysses and the Sirens

Ulysses and his men sailed back to Greece after the Trojan War. They wandered for ten years before Ulysses reached his home. The ship in which Ulysses sailed was rather like a Viking craft. It probably had ten oars a side and one mast with a square sail.

Ulysses had been resting on the Island of Circe. Circe an enchantress, ordered her maid servants to give the Greeks fresh bread and meat and wine to take in their ship She warned Ulysses of the dangers that were ahead of him.

'First of all you will have to pass the island of the Sirens The Sirens have girls' faces and instead of legs they have bird feathers and feet. They will try to bewitch you with their singing. You must make your sailors fill their ears with beeswax so that they don't hear the mysterious music Ulysses, if you want to listen to the music, you must get your crew to tie you to the mast until you are safely past the island.'

Circe told him of other dangers that he would meet. Then Ulysses sailed off at dawn.

Everything happened just as Circe had said.

It was very calm as Ulysses drew near the Sirens' island.
The sail hung down in empty folds so the Greeks lowered it
and started rowing. Ulysses filled their ears with beeswax.
Then they bound him hand and foot to the mast.

Very quietly the music crept over the water. Ulysses
thought it was the most wonderful sound that he had ever
heard. At first it sounded like the wind and the soft swish of
the waves breaking on the shore. Then it became mysterious.
The music grew louder and now Ulysses could hear words;
words which rang in his ears and made him struggle to get
free:

> Stay, O stay, Ulysses!
> Stay, O stay, Ulysses!
> We will teach you the wisdom of the world.
> You will know all the future and the past.

Ulysses shouted and yelled to his men to release him so
that he could dive overboard into the sea and swim to the
island. But they could not hear him. They saw his struggles
and rowed even harder, for they could see that he had been

bewitched by the Sirens. The sailors shouted as they rowed for they felt afraid:

    Row hard, row fast
    Flee, flee from the terrors all around us!

The boat skimmed across the waves and soon Ulysses could no longer hear the music.

This is the rhythm of the Sirens' song:

This is how the tune starts:

Stay,   O   stay   U – lys – ses,

Try to continue it.

The second note of the tune is **F sharp**. This note comes between F and G.

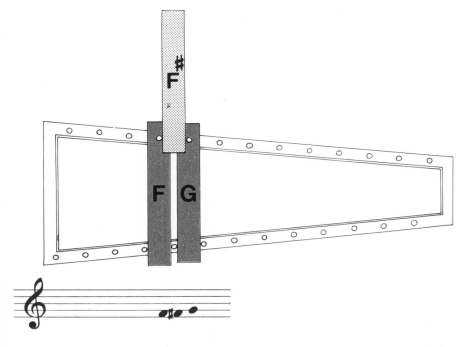

On the stave the sharp sign always comes in front of the note:

In this tune we will use F sharps instead of ordinary Fs all the time. So these are the notes that we can choose from:

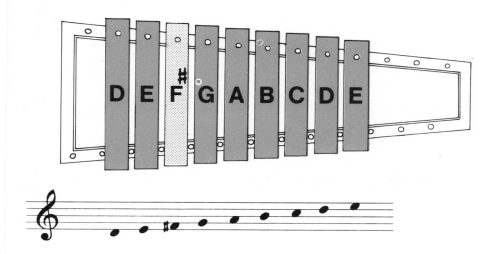

The note F sharp is played on the recorders like this:

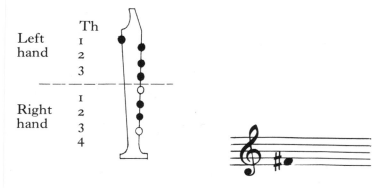

The recorders can join in with the singers when you have written the sirens' tune.

Remember to sing and play it as beautifully as possible, so that we can really imagine what Ulysses heard.

A rhyme

The man in the wilderness asked of me,
How many strawberries grew in the sea.
I answered him as I thought good,
As many red herrings as grew in the wood.

UNKNOWN.

In 1068 Hereward came to England from Flanders. The Normans had invaded England and he wanted to see what had happened to his lands.

He dressed in poor clothes and with his servant arrived at a large house. It was late at night. He was only a mile from his own manor house, but he wanted to hear the news before going home. He knocked at the large door which was bolted and chained. Hereward knew the man who opened the door. It was Osred who had been one of his knights. Osred said that they could stay the night.

The whole household was very sad. The day before a Norman lord had come with many soldiers. They had ordered Hereward's mother to give up all her lands. There had been a fight and Hereward's young brother had been killed and his head chopped off. Hereward was too angry to speak.

As he lay in bed planning what to do, he heard the sound
of noisy singing. It was the Norman lord and his men
singing about their victories.

> We will live in England.
> Drink their wine,
> Eat their food,
> And make the English run.
> And make the English run.

Hereward put on his cloak and with his servant went down
to the village. The singing came from his own house! The
Normans were feasting and drinking. A jester was leaping
and singing.

When Hereward heard the words of the jester's song he
was so furious that his servant had to hold him back.

The jester sang:
Oh! Where is Hereward?
Away across the seas.
Oh! Where is Hereward?
Ah! He has run away.

Hereward snatched a plate of meat from a servant. He walked into the hall, his sword hidden under his cloak. Then with one blow of his sword he killed the Jester. The Normans were too drunk to fight well. Some tried to run but Hereward's servant killed them as they left the hall. Soon they were all dead.

There was great happiness in the village. Soon many more men came to join Hereward and they fought the Normans.

This is the rhythm of the first song:

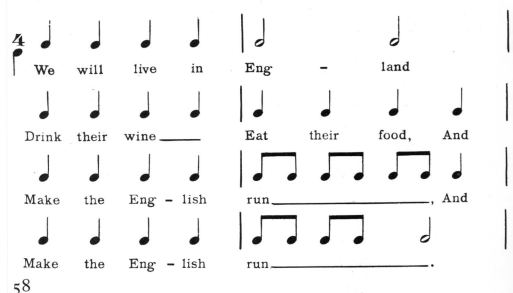

This is the rhythm of the second song:

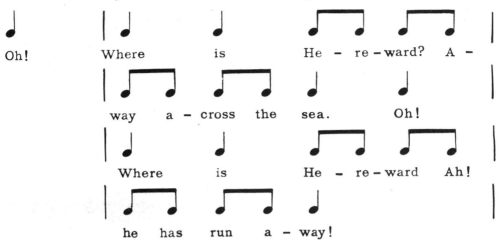

Oh! Where is He – re – ward? A –

way a – cross the sea. Oh!

Where is He – re – ward Ah!

he has run a – way!

These are the notes we can use:

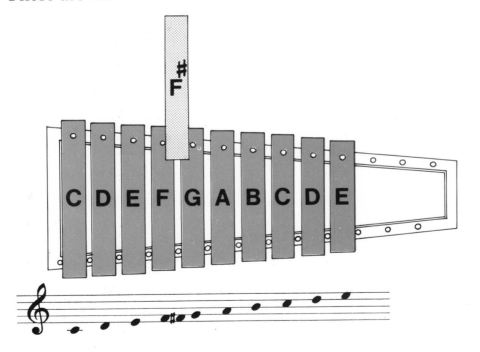

Remember that you do not have to use *all* the notes if you don't want to. Use F *or* F sharp, but not both together.

Don't forget to give your songs an accompaniment. These are some of the rhythms you could use with the first song:

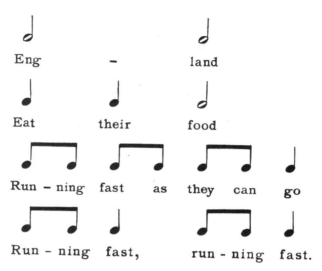

You could use these rhythms with the second song:

Here is a recorder tune that you could use for the villagers
to dance to when Hereward had won:

Make up some rhythms for the accompaniment.

12 The Ice Palace

There was once a strange palace. It was made of ice and shone so beautifully that it could be seen for miles.

The princess sat on her throne and was miserable. This was not surprising. When she was seven the ice witch had cast a spell on her. From that moment the princess could not smile or laugh. The witch had said that if she had not laughed by the time she was eighteen years old, then she would be turned into an icicle. Now she had only a few hours left. At midnight she would be eighteen.

It was all very difficult. When people tried to make her laugh and failed, they were turned into icicles. The palace was full of icicles—tall ones, fat ones, short ones, thin ones. You couldn't move without bumping into an icicle. The King and Queen would have to move out soon, and of course that is just what the ice witch wanted.

There were three brothers who lived nearby. The eldest was very strong; the middle one was very clever and the third one could sing, dance and play lots of musical instruments. The two eldest brothers wanted to make the princess laugh so that they would get a large reward. But the youngest boy just felt very sorry for her. They decided that they must try to break the spell before it was too late.

The three brothers set off for the palace. The strong one carried twenty-seven pigs on his back and he was sure that the princess would think that was funny. The clever one had many books full of funny stories and he was sure the princess would laugh when he read them to her. The youngest

had made up two tunes. The first tune was slow and sad to make the princess cry, but the second tune was fast and bright. It was so jolly that everyone who heard it wanted to dance and sing. He had taught his friends how to play the tunes and they walked behind him carrying their instruments.

So there was quite a long procession going to the palace. The ice witch sat on the roof waiting for midnight to strike. She saw the procession coming but she was not bothered. She had seen so many people coming to the palace and was quite sure that soon they would all be shivering icicles.

What do you think?
Can you make the two tunes for the youngest boy to use in the story?

These are the notes that we can use for the sad tune:

These are the notes that we can use for the jolly tune:

In the first tune it may help if you use lots of long notes. Play them as smoothly as possible. Use a very quiet accompaniment.

In the second song it may help if you use lots of quick notes. The accompaniment must be very jolly too.

64

 # King Lear

Sweet Cherry

Publishing

Published by Sweet Cherry Publishing Limited
Unit E, Vulcan Business Complex,
Vulcan Road,
Leicester, LE5 3EB,
United Kingdom

First published in the UK in 2012
2015 edition

ISBN: 978-1-78226-009-7

©Macaw Books

Title: King Lear

Lexile® code numerical measure L = Lexile® 1140L

Text & Illustrations by Macaw Books 2012

www.sweetcherrypublishing.com

Printed and bound by CPI Group (UK) Ltd, Croydon, CR0 4YY

❧ About ❧
Shakespeare

William Shakespeare, regarded as the greatest writer in the English language, was born in Stratford-upon-Avon in Warwickshire, England (around 23 April 1564). He was the third of eight children born to John and Mary Shakespeare.

Shakespeare was a poet, playwright and dramatist. He is often known as England's national poet and the 'Bard of Avon'. Thirty-eight plays, one hundred and fifty-four sonnets, two long narrative poems and several other poems are attributed to him. Shakespeare's plays have been translated into every major existent language and are performed more often than those of any other playwright.

Cordelia: She is the youngest daughter of King Lear. She is disowned by her father when she refuses to flatter him. She marries the King of France. At the end of the play, she comes to help her father and forgives him for all his ill will towards her.

King Lear: He is the King of Britain. He loves power and flattery, and does not like being contradicted. He wants to enjoy the authority of being king, even though he has unburdened himself of a king's responsibilities.

Goneril: She is the eldest daughter of King Lear and the wife of the Duke of Albany. She flatters her father in order to receive one-third of his kingdom. She is jealous, treacherous and ruthless.

Earl of Kent: He is a nobleman and a loyal subject of King Lear. He disguises himself as Caius when King Lear banishes him, so that he can serve his master. He continues to get himself into trouble throughout the play.

King Lear

Once upon a time, England was ruled by an old and wise king called Lear. King Lear had three daughters – the eldest, Goneril, was married to the Duke of Albany; Regan, his

second daughter, was married
to the Duke of Cornwall; and
his youngest daughter was
called Cordelia, for whom the
King of France and the Duke
of Burgundy were suitors.

After his eightieth birthday,
King Lear felt that it was time
for him to resign from the

matters of the state and spend
the last few years of his life in
other pursuits. So he called
for his three daughters, to
hear from their own lips how
much they loved him. He had
decided that according to their
declarations, he would divide
the kingdom amongst them.

His eldest daughter Goneril had already come to know about his intentions and therefore immediately started proclaiming her love for him in unearthly context. She told him that she loved him more than the light of

her own eyes and that there were no words which could adequately describe her love for him. The king was overjoyed and decided to give her and her husband one-third of his entire kingdom.

After Goneril came Regan. She was one step ahead of her elder sister, and the minute she entered the room and her father asked her how much she loved him, she replied that she loved him much, much more than

Goneril could ever declare. She went on to say that all other joys were dead in comparison to the love that she had for her dear father. Lear was obviously flattered on hearing this, and within an instant he bestowed another third of his kingdom upon her and her husband.

Finally, it was time for Cordelia, his youngest daughter, to enter and declare her love for her father. Now that Lear had already heard his other daughters speak of their love for him, he was sure that Cordelia would love him more

than Goneril and Regan put together. But Cordelia, who had already seen the pretence of her two sisters, merely replied that she loved him as much as she should, no more and no less.

Lear was completely shocked by his daughter's seemingly harsh words, and thinking it was

in jest, he asked her to rethink lest her fortune be marred. But Cordelia was adamant. She said that she loved her father a lot, honoured him and respected him, but once she was married, she would have to share her love with her husband as well. She then went on to ask why, since

both her sisters had made such
tall claims about their love for
their father, they had got married
at all. Surely they
should have stayed
with their father!

In reality,
Cordelia was

the only daughter who loved
Lear to the heights which her
sisters had expressed. But when
she learnt that her sisters had
betrayed their father in order
to acquire his money and that
they did not love him at all,
Cordelia decided that she would

not boast about her love for him,
since she did not care about
his money or his kingdom.

But old age had completely
clouded Lear's sense of reason
and he could not tell the
difference between who loved

him and who did not. He was so
agitated by Cordelia's response
that he immediately withdrew
the third part of the kingdom
he had kept for her and divided
it between Goneril and Regan
and their husbands. He retained
the title of king for himself
and concluded an arrangement

whereby he, along with his one
hundred attendants, would spend
one month in succession at the
castles of his two daughters.

These arrangements seemed
extremely risky to the kingdom,
yet no one had the courage to
defy the king's orders. Only
the Earl of Kent, his most loyal

subject, who cherished him as a
father and honoured him as his
master, spoke up. But this only
stirred the king's wrath even
more. He was so angry with
the Earl of Kent for trying to
defend Cordelia that he at once
banished him from the court.

The earl bade farewell to the king and, hoping that Cordelia would be saved by the gods against the wrongs done to her by her own father, left the court of King Lear forever.

The king then called the Duke of Burgundy and

the King of France to court. He
explained Cordelia's predicament
and how she had come to lose
everything because of her harsh
words. She would now have no
dowry to offer them, and this
information immediately made
the Duke of Burgundy stop
loving Cordelia and he walked off

in a huff, rejecting any further alliance. But the King of France understood what had happened

and said that Cordelia's virtue
and honesty meant much more
to him than any kingdom.
Taking her hand in his, he
asked her to bid farewell to her
sisters and father, and to leave
with him for France, where she
would live as his queen forever.

Cordelia wished
her sisters well, and
asked them to take care
of their father and love
him as much as they had
expressed. The sisters
asked her not to preach
to them and, after a

tearful farewell, Cordelia left for France with her husband-to-be.

Lear's daughters, Goneril and Regan, began to show their true colours within a few days of Cordelia's departure. Lear first noticed this when he was a guest at the house of Goneril. She would feign sickness or pretend

that she was busy whenever her
father tried to talk to her, and
generally make a show of her
displeasure in being bothered
by him. Even the
servants started to
neglect him and
would refuse to
obey his orders.

It did not take King Lear long to understand that all that had been said to him by his daughter was false; she did not love him at all.

However, in the face of such adversity, there are some who have always respected you and cherished your company, and who do their duty once again. Such a man was the Earl of Kent. Though Lear had banished him and said he would be

executed if he were ever found
in Britain again, the earl had not
left. He had stayed to ensure that
the king was safe and taken care
of. So, after disguising himself as
a man by the name of Caius, he
entered the services of the king,

but not for a second did Lear
realise that the man serving him
was the banished Earl of Kent.

Lear had one supporter
left besides Caius: the royal
jester who had stayed loyal to
the king through all his trials

and tribulations. He had kept
the king entertained and tried
to make him smile when he
had lost all reason to do so.

Finally, Goneril came to her father one day and informed him that he was inconveniencing her by staying at her castle for so long and that she wanted him to leave

immediately. As if that were not enough, she also informed him that he should seek company with people who were more his own age and would provide him with better company.

Lear was dumbstruck.

He could not believe that the same Goneril who had showered him with love was now telling him to leave. He immediately ordered his horses to be saddled and decided to leave for Regan's house. He cursed Goneril and wished that she should never have a child, for one day she would

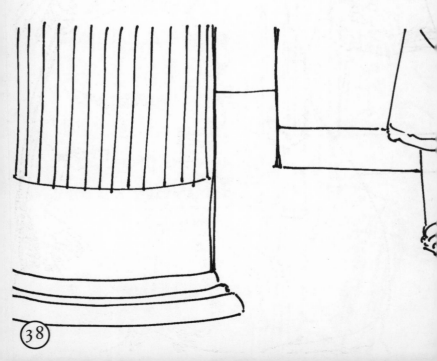

probably even ask the child to
leave. Lear left her castle at once.

Lear asked Caius to go
on ahead and inform Regan
that he was on his way, but it
seemed that Goneril had already
informed Regan about her
father's inconveniencing ways.
She had also asked Regan not to

entertain her father's one hundred
attendants, as she claimed
that they were a nuisance.

When Regan came
to know of this,
though Caius was
a messenger of
King Lear, she
had him locked

up. When Lear arrived at the
castle, the first thing he saw was
his own messenger in chains.
Then he discovered to his utter
dismay that his daughter and
her husband were not even there
to receive him. Upon seeing

how angry he was, they came out at last, but Lear was heartbroken to see that Goneril was with them. Only now was he starting to see the virtue of Cordelia's words.

Regan, as if in a bid to outdo her sister, declared that the one hundred attendants her father had with him were a bit too much and that only twenty-five should stay. This shocked Lear, as he realised that his

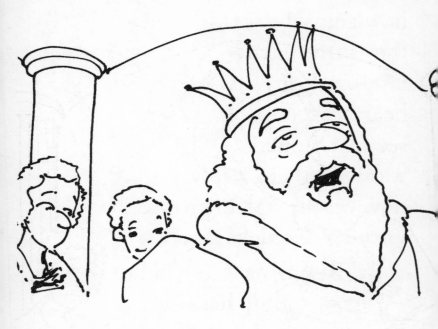

own daughters did not care
about his honour and prestige.
Goneril further commented
that actually he had no need
for any attendants at all.

Lear then decided that under
no circumstances would he enter
either of their castles, and though

a violent storm had begun, he
mounted his horse and set off to
the countryside. Neither of his
daughters tried to stop him.

Even though he took shelter
under a large tree, the poor
king was slashed by the rain.
The jester tried to entreat his
master to return, but Lear was

adamant that he would rather take the evil temperament of nature than beg his daughters to show him any mercy.

Caius, who had been released by Regan's men, found his master and refused to

have him stand there in the storm. He took him to a small hovel, where they could take shelter. There the king saw a beggar, who was lying in the cold with nothing but a blanket over him. Lear remarked to Caius that perhaps he too was a father who had given everything away to his unkind daughters! The poor king seemed to have gone insane.

As the storm subsided, the Earl

of Kent, along with the help
of some of the king's faithful
attendants, took Lear to the
Castle of Dover, where he had
friends. Leaving King

Lear there to be
looked after by
his people, the
earl hastened
to France

to meet Cordelia, now the
Queen of France, and inform
her of her father's condition.
The minute she heard what
had happened, she set off for
Dover at once with the royal
French Army. She had decided
to subdue her sisters and restore
her father's kingdom to him.

Meanwhile, Lear had managed to escape from the castle and run away to the countryside. He was found by Cordelia's entourage stark raving mad, running around singing with a crown of straw on his head. Cordelia's physicians gave him some medication and soon, father and daughter were

reunited. Lear was overjoyed
to see the daughter who really
loved him and asked for her
forgiveness, but Cordelia said that
he had done nothing to require
her forgiveness in the first place.

Meanwhile, the two evil
sisters were having troubles of

their own. They had both fallen
in love with Edward, the Earl of
Gloucester, who had
himself cheated
his brother Edgar
out of his rightful
title. At that time,
Regan's husband,

the Duke of Cornwall, died. Regan immediately decided to marry Edward, but this did not go down well with Goneril, who also wanted to marry him. She poisoned Regan to get her out of the picture, but was caught in

the act. Goneril's
husband, the Duke
of Albany, also
learnt of her love for
the Earl of Gloucester
and put her behind bars.
Unable to bear the humiliation,
Goneril took her own life.

During this time, another tragic event was the death of Cordelia. Regan and Goneril had both sent large armies to meet Cordelia's army, under the leadership of the Earl of Gloucester. Cordelia was captured and decided to end her life in prison by consuming poison. Lear did not live long after receiving news of her death.

Cordelia had lived a full life, for she had even had the opportunity to serve her dear father one last time and all had been resolved between them.

The Earl of Kent, who was also the faithful Caius, could not cope with his master's death. Like the true faithful servant, he followed him to his

grave, perhaps to take care of
his noble master in heaven.

The saga ended when the
evil Edward, the wrongful Earl
of Gloucester, was killed in

battle with his brother Edgar,
the rightful earl. Goneril's
husband, the Duke of Albany,
who had always been averse to
his wife's treatment of her father,

ascended the throne of Britain.
He ruled wisely for many years.